D0712747

Today Is a Windy Day

by Martha E. H. Rustad

CAPSTONE PRESS
a capstone imprint

Pebble Books are published by Capstone Press,
1710 Roe Crest Drive, North Mankato, Minnesota 56003
www.mycapstone.com

Library of Congress Cataloging-in-Publication Data
Cataloging-in-Publication data is on file with the Library of Congress.
ISBN 978-1-5157-4922-6 (library binding)
ISBN 978-1-4966-0945-8 (paperback)
ISBN 978-1-4966-0952-6 (eBook PDF)

Note to Parents and Teachers

The What Is the Weather Today? series supports national
curriculum standards for science related to weather. This book
describes and illustrates a windy day. The images support early
readers in understanding the text. The repetition of words and
phrases helps early readers learn new words. This book also
introduces early readers to subject-specific vocabulary words,
which are defined in the Glossary section. Early readers may need
assistance to read some words and to use the Table of Contents,
Glossary, Read More, Internet Sites, and Index sections of the book.

Printed and bound in the USA.
010060S17

Table of Contents

How's the Weather?

Today is a windy day.

The air moves on a windy day.

Let's find out how windy it is.

Today's Wind Speeds (mph)

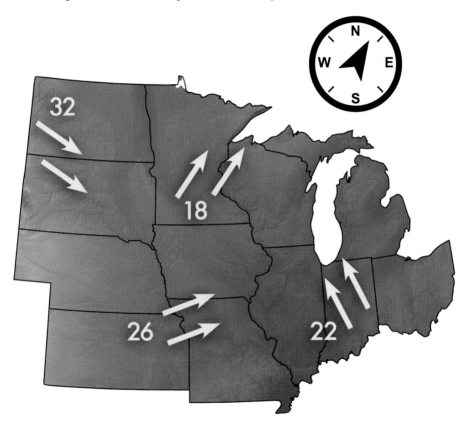

We look at the forecast.
The numbers tell us how
fast the wind will blow.
The arrows tell us the
wind direction.

summer

winter

8

The wind can blow for many days.

Windy days happen in any season.

Warm air blows in the summer.

Cold air blows in the winter.

What Do We See?

We cannot see the wind.

But we can see what the wind moves.

Clouds move quickly across the sky.

Sometimes wind brings in rain clouds.

We see grass and leaves

move in a light wind.

A light wind is called a breeze.

Your hair blows around in the breeze.

Strong winds called gales can bend tree trunks. We see branches move in a strong wind. Flags fly straight out on very windy days.

What Do We Do?

We hang wet clothes outside.

Shirts and pants flap in the wind.

The wind dries out our clothes.

We watch a wind turbine turn.

The wind moves its blades.

This wind energy is turned

into electricity.

We fly a kite on a windy day.

The kite soars above us.

Can we fly a kite tomorrow?

Let's check the forecast.

Glossary

electricity—a form of energy

forecast—a prediction of what the weather will be

pattern—several things that are repeated in the same way several times

turbine—a machine that creates electricity

Read More

Grady, Colin. *Wind Energy.* Saving the Planet through Green Energy. New York, NY: Enslow Publishing, 2017.

Ivancic, Linda. *What Is Wind?* Unseen Science. New York: Cavendish Square, 2016.

VanVoorst, Jenny Fretland. *Wind.* Weather Watch. Minneapolis, MN: Bullfrog Books, 2017.

Internet Sites

FactHound offers a safe, fun way to find Internet sites related to this book. All of the sites on FactHound have been researched by our staff.

Here's all you do:

Visit *www.facthound.com*

Type in this code: 9781515749226

Super-cool stuff! Check out projects, games and lots more at **www.capstonekids.com**

Index

Editorial Credits

Marissa Kirkman, editor; Charmaine Whitman and Peggie Carley, designers; Tracey Engel, media researcher; Katy LaVigne, production specialist

Image Credits

Getty Images: Cultura RM Exclusive/Moof, 8 (bottom), JGI/Daniel Grill, 1, 8 (top); Shutterstock: AlexLinck, 14 (top), andreiuc88, 12; best4u, 6 (compass), Chalermpon Poungpeth, 4, Kseniia Neverkovska, cover and interior design element, Map Resources, 6 (map), Rob Wilson, 14 (bottom), Robnroll, 16, Sergey Novikov, cover, 20, ShaunWilkinson, 10, signet, cover and interior design element, ssuaphotos, 18